Langston Hughes

Illustrated by Gary Kelley

Aunt Sue's Stories

Creative Editions

Aunt Sue has a head full of stories.
Aunt Sue has a whole
heart full of stories.

Summer nights on the front porch
Aunt Sue cuddles a
brown-faced child to her bosom
And tells him stories.

Black slaves
Working in the hot sun,

And black slaves
Walking in the dewy night,

And black slaves

Singing sorrow songs on the banks of a mighty river

Mingle themselves softly
In the flow of old Aunt Sue's voice,
Mingle themselves softly
In the dark shadows that cross and recross
Aunt Sue's stories.

And the dark-faced child, listening,
Knows that Aunt Sue's stories are real stories.
He knows that Aunt Sue
Never got her stories out of any book at all,
But that they came
Right out of her own life.

And the dark-faced child is quiet
Of a summer night
Listening to Aunt Sue's stories.

James Mercer Langston Hughes was born in Joplin, Missouri, in 1901. His father abandoned the family shortly after Langston's birth, and he was raised primarily by his grandmother, Mary Leary Langston, in Lawrence, Kansas. Following her death in 1915, Langston lived first with family friends in Kansas, and then moved to Illinois and Ohio before traveling and working abroad. Eventually, he made his way to Harlem, where he established a lifelong profession for himself as a writer. He strove to represent Black people as they were, challenging the racial stereotypes that permeated American society of the 1920s and beyond. Beloved as much as he was criticized, Langston constantly experimented with form and voice, infusing his early poetry with the rhythms of jazz, then the polemics of socialism, before turning to satire, children's books, translations, and any other literary work that would provide income. By the time of his death in 1967, he had returned to utilizing his art in thought-provoking ways while reaffirming his bedrock belief that all Americans should be included in the democratic ideals established for some.

Illustrations copyright © 2024 by Gary Kelley / Designed by Rita Marshall / Published in 2024 by Creative Editions / P. O. Box 227, Mankato, MN 56002 USA Creative Editions is an imprint of The Creative Company / www.thecreativecompany.us / All rights reserved. No part of the contents of this book may be reproduced by any means without the written permission of the publisher. Printed in China / **Library of Congress Cataloging-in-Publication Data** / Names: Hughes, Langston, 1902–1967, author. / Kelley, Gary, 1945–, illustrator. Title: Aunt Sue's stories / by Langston Hughes; illustrated by Gary Kelley. Description: Mankato, Minnesota : Creative Editions, 2024. / Audience: Ages 7–9. / Audience: Grades 2–3. / Summary: An illustrated picture book of Langston Hughes's classic 1926 poem about a Black boy listening to a relative's shadow-crossed stories of slavery honors a culture's history keepers. Identifiers: LCCN 2023013363 (print) / LCCN 2023013364 (ebook) / ISBN 9781568464039 (hardcover) / ISBN 9781568464046 (pdf) Subjects: LCSH: Children's poetry, American. / African Americans—Juvenile poetry. / Slavery—United States—Juvenile poetry. / CYAC: American poetry. / African Americans—Poetry. / Slavery—Poetry. / LCGFT: Poetry. Classification: LCC PS3515.U274 A96 2024 (print) / LCC PS3515.U274 (ebook) / DDC 811/.54—dc23/eng/20230424 LC record available at https://lccn.loc.gov/2023013363 / LC ebook record available at https://lccn.loc.gov/2023013364

First edition 9 8 7 6 5 4 3 2 1